She Set the Sky Ablaze

Nico Solheim-Davidson

Three Drops Press
Sheffield, United Kingdom

First published in 2018 by Three Drops Press

Three Drops Press
Sheffield, United Kingdom

www.threedropspoetry.co.uk

ISBN 978-0-244-71906-7

"blessed be
she
who is
both
furious
and
magnificent"
— Taylor Rhodes, calloused: a field journal

"She will rise. With a spine of steel and a roar like thunder, she will rise."
— Nicole Lyons

Introduction

Since my younger years as a child, I've always had a love for mythology – beginning with Greek myths such as the twelve trials of Heracles and the Trojan War to Nordic myths such as Odin's quests for knowledge and Thor battling the Midgard Serpent.

As I've grown older, I've found more appreciation for the female figures in the myths such as Freyja, Victoria, the Morrigan and others. **She Set The Sky Ablaze** is a collection of my poems inspired by the ladies that appear in the myths of pre-Christian Europe.

It has been a fun experience for me, writing the poems that are in this book as well as reading about the various goddesses and other ladies of European mythology.

The pieces within the book cover Celtic, Nordic, Baltic, Slavic, and Graeco-Roman mythology. Some figures will be easy to recognise within the book and others are more obscure.

Morrigan

The Mother of War
Threads the web of Fate
Scarlet clouds follow
Where Death's crone does walk
Beauty, Hag and Crow
In battle's heat she reigns
Phantom Queen of Doom
Upon raven wings
Dark words she carries

Sinann's Folly

To Connla's Well, she journeyed
In spite of the omens, dark
For t'was wisdom she sought
And wisdom she found
For the wise salmon, she caught
And the wise salmon, she ate
But the omen's truth came
As the Well spilled its water
And to the sea, she was taken

Raven-Hearted Queen

War and death, bound to her
by wings of starless night
Beneath her lunar gaze
Conquest she does decree
Queen with the Raven Heart

Birthing of the Boyne

Against her husband's command
She approached the well
Surrounded by hazels
Where wise salmon thrived
The well's power, she challenged
As widdershins, we walked
Hysterically, the waters soared,
towards the blessed sea
Claiming on their march
Her anointed soul

Dubh's Pool

By jealous rage, blinded
The Druidess weaved the spell
that would drown her rival
But to her horror,
through foolish angst,
Her husband's death
She also wrought

Shieldmaiden

There she stood,
Within the storm,
Battle born,
A daughter of Freyja
In her soul
Thor's thunder roars,
And in her eyes
Sparks that set
The sky ablaze

Sigrun

The flame-haired maiden,
Named for Victory's rune,
Held in battle's soul
Upon her death-bed,
To the halls of War's true lord
Born a Valkyrie
The wild storm's spirit
With bloodkin, new, in Death's hall
Choosers of the slain
For night alone,
With a heart full of passion
She laid with her love

Skadi

Winter and death follow
The Ice-crowned huntress
In her sunless wake
Through the mountains,
She travels, in ominous snow-shoes
And in her frigid heart
Where wintertide thunders
The snow never melts

Nótt

The masker, thrice wed,
Who brings the joy-of-sleep,
Before the Day, her son, she rides
Around Jord, the earth, that she birthed
She is Darkness and the Night,
Eternal Dream Goddess

Hildr

From Death, feeders of ravens
She summons back to the fields
Of the meeting of swords
To maintain the storm that rages
Between Hogni and Heginn
Until the winters of three comes

Eir

Our blood-snakes clash
And a crow's feast, served
As the sky grows dark
And Mani's tears fall
She walks the battle-harbour
Without angst nor fear
Upon our wounded men
Healing charms, she leaves
And those whom flame-farewelled
She guides to Odin's Hall

Gunnr

The Swan of Blood
Around the fields, flies
She gives sleep of the sword
to those who would meet
The Lord of the Gallows

Mist

She dances through the air
Like a snow flake in the wind
Her armour, shines like Sol,
As she rides to battle's field

The Mountain and The Sea

In the hall
Where Summer's waves
Did kiss the land
Nine nights she spent
But no more

The mountains she missed
And the howling of wolves
In the veil of night

She was a Maid of Winter
Wedded to a Summer lord
But her heart yearned
For the icy caress
Of her mountain halls

Half-Corpse Queen

In northern lands,
Where the living dwell not,
In her hall, she reigns
This Half-Corpse Queen
Here where even Asgard defies her, not
The dark nights, her gown,
and the grim winters, her bed
In the north, 'til Ragnarok
Her's is the throne

Dawn Star

As the night's cold veil descends,
Upon the island, where the sun dwells,
The palace gates, she opens
Before battle's field, she wanders
To guard her favoured champions

Evening Star

When the day's reign ends, as the sun returns
The palace gates she closes, as night ascends
She guards the Doom-bearing hound
Sister of Dawn's star, betrothed of the moon

Morana

As the Winter comes howling,
From Death's realm, she ascends
This Queen of Frozen Ruin
Night's mare she invokes
through the shadow months
Until the Spring breaks through the dawn
And her body withers upon the pyre

Breksta

Oh Twilight Empress
Who guards me as I sleep
She brings dreams of fortune, great
Prophecies set in stone

As Saule slumbers
And the stars glimmer so
The night's veil she wanders
Musings of joy, she weaves

She is the breaking dawn
And the dusk which is falling
The Guardian of Dreamers
And from dusk to dawn, her vigil lasts

She-Wolf

Night blankets the world
As the moon rises
The Lycanthropic Queen
Leads her graceful pack
through the forests they guard
The Hunter's scent, she tracks
And a Hare, she sends
For him, an omen
Should he linger

Gabija

Crowned with embers
And cloaked in flaming scarlet
In the hearth, she dances
Until the night falls
And then, 'neath the ashes
She slumbers 'til the dawning

Death Becomes Her

A maiden, so divine
Her beauty, alluring
Until that came
beneath a pine drape
When she did awake
for seven years, trapped!
And as the eighth began
from that sober crypt
Like bitter mist, she rose
A maiden, no more
But a monster, deformed
A bane, a blight to all mortals
Death becomes Her...

Mother Sun

Mother crowned in Heaven
The blazing life-giver
From her throne on high
For the foundlings, she cares
And heart and warmth
She gives them

Amber Tears

Across storm-ridden waves
Her sorrowed voice echoes
Where the crest meets the shore
Her amber tears crown the strand
Evermore, her love, she mourns

Queen Egle

With no thought for consequence
In folly, she pledged her hand
To the serpentine of human tongue
So her clothing, she could reclaim

But Saule thrice rose and fell
Before the slithering legion came
To claim the maiden, young Egle
For their Prince 'neath the tides

Yet the Ophidian Prince
Stood not as a serpentine
But as a man, of vast beauty
And her husband, he would be

Three sons and a daughter
She bore him, their fated storm
For one would betray her
When blood meets with kin

Her kin, Egle wished to see,
But her wishes, the Prince denied
Lest three feats, ever hopeless
She could replete in full

But with a Sorcerer's aid
Iron boots, she wore down
The endless silky tuft, she spun
And a pie baked without the means

Her family, long lost, bright to see her
But to the sea, in the west,
her return, they bequested not
And a guileful plot they made

To lure Egle's Prince to land,
Her three sons, briskly, they lashed
But his secret, not theirs to say
And in dread, the girl spoke all

And when the butchery did wane
To her fallen Prince, Egle called
Athwart the Western tides
Greeted only by sanguine fluid

With hope dashed, anguish rose
Ash, Oak and Birch, her sons became
And the daughter, an aspen shaking
So after, as a spruce, Egle stood

Death

She is Death
the pale shadow
that lingers
at your pallet's head

She is Death
the owl's calling
in the Witching Hour
as you slumber

She is Death
the shade that wanders
through the eternal home
and on the late, feeds

She is Death
and the ending kiss
As down your throat
Her baneful tongue crawls

Ave Victoria

Legions clash as the dawn breaks,
Steel and bone entwined
as flesh torn asunder
Amidst the storm of blood
and dying breaths
there she stands,
Roma's Golden protector
Upon her shield and laurel leaves,
The battle is won
My name I see
Her gift to me, bestowed,
With sword in hand,
The winged diva I hail,
AVE VICTORIA!

She Is Fire, Earthly and Divine

Cloaked in a sea of flames
In Rome's hearth, she stands
Queen of eternal inferno
Life's enkindler, earth itself
Whose true, noble cast
in the flare is hidden
Veiled with embers divine
to remain unsullied
As her pure allure
would wither mortal eyes

Oceanid

Serene and mysterious
Like the ever-changing ocean
Her voice, a siren's song
Enchanting, alluring
Her heart, a river
Finds its way
To tides she commands

The Night's Lover

Dark mist crowns her head
Emblazoned with distant stars
From eventide's passing to Hemara's rising
She reigns high in Heaven
Nyx, my heart's desire

From Hades she ascends
Upon Stygian wings
Crepuscular, her domain
As shades of dusk, she leaves
Painted in her wake
Honest is my love for Nyx

Ever fearsome in her wrath
Even Olympus quakes before her
The Mother of Sleep and Death
And dreams and Fate she birthed
From her sunless womb
Oh sable Nyx, I long for you

As dawn breaks in eastern lands,
Led by majestic Apollo,
Her reign comes to an end
And I am left waiting
To embrace Nyx once more
Within her darkened hall

Bolina – The Sun's Beloved

The Maiden fair, but mortal,
Desired by the Solar Lord,
Into Poseidon's realm,
From upon high, she cast her being,
But Apollo, so infatuated,
Deified the Maiden fair,
As a Queen of the Waves

Chthonian River

Between Death's kingdom
and fields of the Living
She endured 'til time's end
From her Molten womb,
Zeal and Victory, she spawned
State and Violence, she bore
Oaths, upon her, by Regal Olympus
She is Hatred and the river, immortal

The Huntress and the River

The River fell for her
But driven mad by desire
Tried, with force, to claim her
But wise, the Huntress is,
With mud, her face, she hid
So the River would find her not

Enchantress

Hekate's kin, the Sun's blood,
Crowned, A Queen of Witchcraft
Upon the island, she dwells
Exiled here, for her husband's death
With only her banes
As wicked beasts, turned
For companionship

Lady of Athens

With her kin, she competed
For the city's unpledged heart,
Where he offered salt and water,
She promised the Olive's tree,
A Gift that won the city's heart

Gorgon

A beautiful maiden was she,
whom pledged herself to Athena,
With a celibate's vow, as a Priestess,
And her heart, so full of joy

But the ocean's Lord lusted for her,
And his advances she would deny,
Athena's service she was within
And that oath, she would not betray

Then the fateful day would come,
When the Ocean's Lord would claim,
With force and rage, that which was not his
Her innocence, her purity, violated

Soon Athena learned, of that grim crime,
that unhallowed her Temple grounds
Her fury, she would unleash, ever so vile
Upon her Priestess, so loyal

And so, the Priestess, once so beautiful,
Was morphed from maiden to Beast,
Snakes now grew, where her hair once was
And her legs, a python's scaly body

Vilified for a crime, which hers was not,
From Athens, she fled, to lands distant
Sorrow took root in her heart
But soon to be replaced by venomous fury

Vengeance, she swore against Athena
Against the Ocean's Lord and Olympus
For her curse gave the means of revenge
"Hell hath no fury, like the Gorgon scorned!"

The Huntress and the River

The River fell for her
But driven mad by desire
Tried, with force, to claim her
But wise, the Huntress is,
With mud, her face she hid,
So the River would find her not

Lady of the Crossroads

Upon the crossroads
She rules the moon and the night
This Queen of Witches

Born from Titan's blood
Daughter of the Starry skies
Draped in pale moonlight

From Grand Olympus
Honour sent by Deathless Gods
She receives in large

To Demeter's kin
A minister and a friend
In dusky Hades

Of three realms she rules
The Heavens, Earth and Hades
Her lands from of old

Hekate, her name
Lady of the Trivium,
Of Death and witchcraft

She Is The Hunt

She is the arrow,
From the hunter's bow, loosed,
That finds its target

She is the Wild Queen,
Daughter of the Thunder
And Sun's graceful twin

She is nature supreme
The predator hunting prey
That which brings blood and birth

She is the hunt!
The scent of blood and death
That lingers on the wind

Acknowledgements

First, I would like to thank the 9562* Yorkshire Tea bags that valiantly sacrificed their lives so that I might keep awake during in the "long" process of writing this book.

A special thank you to Kat and Vytaute, as well, as well as Peter of the metal band Skyforger, for your help with my research into the mythology of the Baltic people has been most valuable to me.

Thanks to Mike Sheriff for the cover art.

Also, a very special thank you to Kate and the rest of the Three Drops team for taking an interest in *She Set The Sky Ablaze*, and of course, for publishing it.

And of course, a thank you to you, the reader, for taking an interest in my work.

**It's probably closer to 600 but who's counting?*